Men's Cook

Men Can Cook Delicious Meals Too

BY

Rachael Rayner

License Notes

No part of this Book can be reproduced in any form or by any means including print, electronic, scanning or photocopying unless prior permission is granted by the author.

All ideas, suggestions and guidelines mentioned here are written for informative purposes. While the author has taken every possible step to ensure accuracy, all readers are advised to follow information at their own risk. The author cannot be held responsible for personal and/or commercial damages in case of misinterpreting and misunderstanding any part of this Book

Table of Contents

Introduction

Those who cook know how money saving it is to enjoy good food at home as opposed to throwing hundreds of bucks in restaurants every day. If you are new to cooking, you may get overwhelmed as there are so many cuisines and several techniques of cooking. But we know men like to cook fast, hassle free and delicious food. To achieve all of these three things, we come to you with this fabulous cookbook. It contains 30 delicious dishes that every man would love. We know men love meat, especially beef.

The books contain a lot of beef recipes and chicken recipes. For the vegetable lovers out there, there are some finger-licking veggie dishes too.

You will find breakfast, brunch, lunch, dinner recipes that are super delicious. They take very little, almost no prep to make them. The Ingredients that have been used in this book are very common and found in almost everywhere around the world. So, no need to go on a hunt while grocery shopping.

Make these recipes yourself and see how homemade food tastes much better.

Brunch Sandwich

Men love skipping breakfast. Although it is not recommended but let's be real, most man living alone enjoys brunch more often. This is a simple and quick high protein brunch sandwich.

Serving Size: 1

Serving Size: 10 Minutes

Ingredients:

- 1 egg
- ½ cup sliced sausage
- 2 tbsp mayo
- 1 tbsp tomato ketchup
- 2 lettuce leaves
- 2 tomato slices
- 1 tsp butter
- Salt and pepper to taste
- 2 bread slices

Instruction:

Water-poach the egg in the microwave.

In a pan add some butter and fry the sausage for 2 minutes.

Toast the bread slices. Spread the tomato ketchup and mayo onto the bread.

Assemble the sandwich with tomato slices, lettuce leaves, sausage and egg.

Enjoy.

Creamy Chicken Shell Pasta

Pasta is your ultimate comfort food. But men cannot have it simple. They need it to be cheesy and meaty!

Serving Size: 2

Serving Size: 20 Minutes

Ingredients:

- 1 lb. shell pasta
- 1 cup minced chicken
- 1 cup grated cheddar cheese
- 1 tsp paprika
- 1 cup heavy cream
- Salt and pepper to taste
- 1 tsp oregano
- 1 tbsp butter
- 2 tbsp tomato sauce

Instruction:

Boil the pasta 10 minutes in salted water. Drain and set aside for now.

In a skillet, melt the butter. Add the minced chicken.

Toss for 2 minutes. Add the tomato sauce, oregano, salt, pepper, paprika and toss for a minute.

Add the heavy cream and cook for 3 minutes.

Add the boiled shells and stir for 2 minutes.

Add the cheese and cook for 3 minutes. Serve hot.

Spicy Creamy Shrimp Curry

This is a spicy seafood curry which will leave you licking your fingers after you relish it. It is delicious and looks ravishingly vibrant.

Serving Size: 2

Serving Size: 15 Minutes

Ingredients:

- 1 lb. medium shrimp, skin removed, deveined
- 1 can coconut milk
- 1 green chili, chopped
- 1 red chili, chopped
- Salt and pepper to taste
- 1 tsp red chili powder
- 1 garlic clove, minced
- 1 tsp minced ginger
- 1 tbsp olive oil
- Fresh chives, chopped

Instruction:

In a pan, add the oil and fry the garlic and ginger.

Add the coconut milk, red chili powder, salt, pepper, and cook for 5 minutes.

Add the shrimp, red chili, green chili and chives.

Cook for 5 minutes. Serve hot.

Chicken with beans and veggies

This is a one pot meal which can be made in pressure cooker, or instant cooker. I have sued pressure cooker here so it took less time. The beans, the carrot and corn complement the chicken quite well.

Serving Size: 2

Serving Size: 15 Minutes

Ingredients:

- 2 chicken breasts, diced
- ½ cup sliced carrots
- ½ cup diced tomatoes
- 2 cup chicken stock
- ½ cup corn kernels
- 1 can black beans, drained
- Salt and white pepper to taste
- Fresh parsley, chopped, to serve

Instruction:

In a pressure cooker, add the chicken pieces.

Add the chicken stock. Add all the veggies.

Add the salt, pepper and cover. Cook for 20 minutes.

Serve hot with parsley on top.

Herby Penne Pasta

Pasta tastes good as it is, but when you add two types of cheese in it, it becomes heavenly. **Serving Size:** 2

Serving Size: 20 Minutes

Ingredients:

- 1 lb. penne pasta
- 1 cup cheddar cheese, grated
- ½ cup grated parmesan
- Salt to taste
- Pepper to taste
- 1 tsp oregano
- 1 cup milk
- 1 tbsp flour
- 2 tbsp butter
- 3 garlic cloves, minced
- 1 green chili, chopped
- Fresh parsley, chopped, to serve

Instruction:

Boil the pasta for 10 minutes in salted water. Drain and set aside.

In a nonstick pan, melt the butter. Add the flour and toss for 2 minutes.

Add the milk and stir for 5 minutes.

Add the cheddar cheese and parmesan cheese.

Add salt, pepper, garlic, oregano and chili.

Add the boiled pasta and toss for 5 minutes. Add parsley on top and serve hot.

Spicy Chicken

Men like their meat spicy. This is very spicy chicken curry which tastes great with rice or any type of bread.

Serving Size: 2

Serving Size: 30 Minutes

Ingredients:

- 1 lb. chicken
- 2 cup chicken stock
- 1 cup diced onion
- 1 green chili
- Fresh coriander, chopped
- Salt to taste
- 1 tbsp ginger garlic paste
- 1 tsp paprika
- 1 tsp red chili powder
- 1 tsp cumin
- 2 tbsp mustard oil

Instruction:

Cut the chicken into medium pieces.

In a large pan, heat the mustard oil. Fry the onion for 4 minutes.

Add the ginger garlic paste and 2 tbsp chicken stock.

Add all the spices and pour in the stock.

Cook for 5 minutes on high heat.

Add the chicken pieces. Stir for 2 minutes.

Cover and cook for 15 minutes.

Add coriander and serve hot.

Broccoli and Chicken

This dish would leave you begging for more! The texture of the chicken is crunchy and the sauce is kind of sweet and yet spicy.

Serving Size: 2

Serving Size: 30 Minutes

Ingredients:

- 1 lb. chicken breasts

- 1 cup broccoli florets, diced

- 1 cup chicken stock

- 2 white onion, diced

- 2 green chilies

- 1 tsp minced garlic

- 1 tsp paprika

- 1 tbsp soy sauce

- 1 tbsp tomato sauce

- 1 tbsp olive oil

- 2 tbsp flour

- 1 tbsp mixed herbs

- Oil for frying chicken

Instruction:

Cut the chicken breasts into medium chunks.

Combine the flour, salt, pepper, and paprika in a bowl.

Coat the chicken pieces in the flour mix.

Fry the chicken golden brown. Transfer to a kitchen paper.

In a large pot, heat the olive oil.

Add the onion and cook for 2 minutes. Add the soy sauce, tomato sauce, stock, paprika, salt, pepper, garlic, mixed herbs, and mix well. Cook on high heat for 5 minutes.

Add the broccoli and the chicken pieces. Cook for another 5 minutes.

Serve hot.

Beef Mushroom Carrot Stew

When you combine beef with carrot, the sweetness from the carrot tenderizes the meat. Adding the mushroom in the stew adds a different layer to the simple dish.

Serving Size: 2

Serving Size: 50 Minutes

Ingredients:

- 1 lb. beef, cut into medium pieces
- 1 cup thickly sliced carrot
- ½ cup peas
- 1 cup button mushroom
- Salt and black pepper to taste
- 1 tbsp ginger paste
- 1 tbsp garlic paste
- 1 tsp cumin
- 1 tsp turmeric
- 2 tsp red chili powder

- 1 tsp coriander

- 4 cup beef stock

Instruction:

In a pressure cooker, add the beef, and the stock.

Cover and cook on high heat for 20 minutes.

Add the carrot, mushroom, the spices and pastes.

Stir well and cover again. Cook on medium heat for 20 minutes.

Add the peas and cook for another 10 minutes. Serve hot.

Cauliflower Tomato Curry

Meat dishes are fine but men also need to eat vegetarian dishes once in a while. This is one such vegetarian dish that tastes so good that you hardly miss meat!

Serving Size: 2

Serving Size: 20 Minutes

Ingredients:

- 1 cup cauliflower florets, diced
- 1 cup diced potatoes
- 1 cup tomatoes, diced
- 1 green chili
- 1 cup yogurt
- 1 tsp pepper
- Salt to taste
- ¼ tsp turmeric
- 1 tbsp butter
- 1 cup peas

Instruction:

In a pan, melt the butter, put the garlic and cook until golden brown.

Add the cauliflower, potatoes and cook for 5 minutes.

Add the peas, tomatoes, green chili, turmeric, salt and pepper.

Cook for 5 minutes. Pour in the yogurt. Stir for 5 minutes.

Serve hot.

Beef Potato Curry

Men love meat and combing meat with potato makes a dish finger licking good. If you do not have to worry about the carbohydrates, then serve this dish with rice. It will blow your mind.

Serving Size: 2

Serving Size: 1 hour

Ingredients:

- 1 lb. beef, with bones, cut into medium pieces

- 1 cup diced potatoes

- 4 cup water

- 1 tsp cumin

- 1 tsp red chili powder

- ½ cup diced onion

- 4 garlic cloves, minced

- 2 inch ginger, minced

- 1 tsp paprika

- 1 dried red chili

- 2 tbsp oil

- Salt to taste

- 1 black cardamom

- 1 star anise

- 1 bay leaf

- 1 cinnamon stick

- 1 tsp chopped rosemary

Instruction:

In a pot, heat the oil. Fry the potatoes golden brown.

Transfer to a plate. In the same pan, sear the beef. Transfer to a plate.

Add the ginger and garlic. Stir for 3 minutes. Put the onion and cook for 2 minutes.

Add the spices, herbs and 1 cup water.

Cover and cook for 5 minutes. Add the beef and stir well. Cook on high heat for 20 minutes.

Add the potatoes and cook for 10 minutes.

Pour in the water and cook on high heat for 30 minutes. Serve hot.

Chicken and Spinach Curry

Serving Size: 2

Serving Size: 30 Minutes

Ingredients:

- 1 lb. chicken, cut into 8 pieces
- 2 cup spinach
- 2 cup chicken stock
- 1 cup heavy cream
- 1 tsp turmeric
- 1 tsp red chili powder
- Salt and pepper to taste
- 1 onion, diced
- 1 cardamom
- 1 cinnamon stick
- 2 tbsp butter
- 1 tsp garlic powder
- 1 tsp ginger powder

- ½ tsp mixed herbs

Instruction:

In a skillet, heat the oil. Fry the chicken pieces golden brown. Transfer them to a plate.

Add the onion and cook for 1 minute. Add the ginger, garlic powder, cinnamon stick, cardamom, red chili powder, turmeric, salt and pepper.

Add 2 tbsp stock and cook for 5 minutes. Return the chicken and cook for 8 minutes.

Add the remaining stock and cook for 5 minutes. Add the spinach, mixed herbs and heavy cream. Cook for 5 minutes. Serve hot.

Mutton Paella

This mutton paella is a festive dish. When there is a special occasion, men can throw this in a pot and have one side dish and they will be covered to present a fabulous lunch of dinner party.

Serving Size: 2

Serving Size: 1 hour

Ingredients:

- 1 lb. mutton
- 2 cup long grain rice
- 4-6 jalapeno peppers
- Salt to taste
- 1 cup sliced onion
- ½ tsp saffron
- 2 tbsp warm milk
- 1 cup yogurt
- 1 tbsp soy sauce
- 1 tsp cumin

- 1 tbsp ginger paste

- 1 tbsp garlic paste

- 1 tbsp lemon juice

- 3 tbsp oil

Instruction:

Cut the mutton pieces into medium chunks. Marinate the mutton with salt, ginger garlic paste, soy sauce, lemon juice yogurt, and cumin. Let it sit for half an hour.

Fry the onion golden brown in oil. Transfer to a paper towel.

Soak the saffron in warm water for 10 minutes.

Cook the rice in salted water for only 5 minutes. Drain and rinse well.

In a large pot, add the mutton with it marinated juice.

Add the boiled rice on top. Add the fried onion, jalapeno pepper and saffron mix.

Cover. Cook on medium low heat for 40 minutes. Serve hot.

Lentil Curry

When you are feeling lazy, you can opt for this dish. It is simple and tasty.

Serving Size: 2

Serving Size: 25 Minutes

Ingredients:

- 1 cup lentil

- 1 cup diced tomatoes

- Fresh basil, chopped

- ¼ tsp turmeric

- Salt to taste

- 2 green chilies

- 4 cup water

Instruction:

In a pressure cooker, add the lentils.

Add the water, salt, turmeric, tomatoes and cook for 20 minutes.

Add the chilies, and basil. Cook for 5 minutes. Serve hot.

Green Chicken with Veggies

When you are tired of the traditional dishes, try this one out. The green flavors of the chicken and veggies would impress you.

Serving Size: 2

Serving Size: 30 Minutes

Ingredients:

- 1 lb. chicken cut into pieces. Bones removed
- 1 cup diced bell pepper
- 1 cup diced carrot
- 1 cup diced zucchini
- Salt and white pepper to taste
- 2 cup chicken stock
- 2 green chilies
- ¼ cup chopped coriander
- ¼ cup chopped scallions
- 1 white onion, diced

- 2 garlic cloves, minced

- 2 tbsp butter

- 2 peppercorns

Instruction:

In a blender, add the green chilies with coriander and scallion. Add the garlic and blend for 1 minute.

In a pan, melt the butter. Add the onion and fry for a minute.

Add the chili mixture. Add the peppercorns, and chicken.

Toss for 5 minutes and add the veggies. Stir for 4 minutes.

Pour in the stock and cook for 10 minutes. Add the salt and cook for 2 minutes.

Serve hot.

BBQ Ribs

This sticky rib is simple to make and takes little prep behind it. If you are having a game night, it will serve you great.

Serving Size: 2

Serving Size: 40 Minutes

Ingredients:

- 1 lb. rib, cut into medium pieces
- ½ cup brown sugar
- 1 tbsp BBQ sauce
- 1 tbsp soy sauce
- Black pepper to taste
- 1 tbsp mixed herbs
- 1 tsp garlic powder
- 2 tbsp olive oil
- Parsley, to serve

Instruction:

Preheat the oven to 400 degrees F., place aluminum foil on a baking tray.

Combine the brown sugar, BBQ sauce, mixed herbs, olive oil, garlic powder, pepper, and soy sauce. Mix well and marinate the ribs for 2 hours.

Arrange them on a baking tray. Bake for 20 minutes.

Turn them over and bake for 20 minutes again. Serve hot with parsley on top.

Pumpkin Tofu Curry

If you are a vegetarian, it is a delightful dish to serve with rice. Very nutritional and quick to make!

Serving Size: 2

Serving Size: 20 Minutes

Ingredients:

- 1 cup diced pumpkin
- 1 cup diced extra firm tofu
- 1 cup heavy cream
- 1 cup spinach
- Salt to taste
- 1 tbsp tomato sauce
- 1 tbsp ginger paste
- 1 tbsp garlic paste
- 1 tsp red chili powder
- ¼ tsp turmeric
- 2 tbsp oil

- 1 onion, sliced

Instruction:

In a pan, heat the oil and fry the onion.

Add the gigner paste, garlic paste and 2 tbsp water. Stir well and cook for 1 minute.

Put the tofu and fry until golden brown.

Add the pumpkin, turmeric, red chili powder and salt.

Toss for 4 minutes. Add the spinach and cook for 2 mintues.

Add the heavy cream, tomato sauce and cook for 5 mintues. Serve hot with rice.

Creamy Vegetarian Stew

Vegetarian curry goes really well with rice. A squeeze of fresh lemon juice and fresh herbs increases the flavors.

Serving Size: 2

Serving Size: 20 Minutes

Ingredients:

- 1 cup diced cauliflower floret
- 1 cup sliced carrots
- 1 cup diced shiitake mushroom
- Fresh parsley, chopped
- 1 tbsp lemon juice
- 1 cup heavy cream
- 2 garlic cloves, minced
- 1 tbsp butter
- 1 cup vegetable stock
- Salt to taste
- White pepper to taste

- 1 tbsp tomato sauce

- 1 tbsp chopped lemongrass

- 2 peppercorns

- 1 green chili, chopped

Instruction:

In a large pot, add the butter. Add the lemongrass, and garlic.

Cook for 2 minutes. Add the vegetables and cook for 5 minutes.

Add the rest of the ignredients. Stir well and cook for 10 minutes.

Serve hot.

Fish in Tomato Gravy

Have you ever tried fish in tomato gravy? The sweetness of the tomatoes and the spice s brings so many layers to this simple fish dish.

Serving Size: 2

Serving Size: 25 Minutes

Ingredients:

- 1 lb. ruhu fish

- 1 cup tomato puree

- Salt to taste

- Pepper to taste

- Fresh coriander, chopped

- 1 tsp red chili powder

- ¼ tsp turmeric

- 1 tsp cumin

- 1 tsp coriander powder

- 1 tsp ginger paste

- 1 tsp garlic paste

- 1 cup coconut milk

Instruction:

Cut the fish into medium chunks. Marinate the fish pieces with turmeric and some salt.

In a pan heat the oil and fry the fish golden brown from both sides.

Transfer to a plate. In the same pan, add the onion. Toss for 1 minute.

Add the ginger paste and garlic paste. Add 2 tbsp water. Cook for 2 minutes.

Add the dry spices and cook for 2 minutes. Add the tomato puree and coconut milk and bring it to boil.

Add the fish and cook for 10 minutes. Serve hot.

Pan fried Cow Kidney

As bizarre it may sound, cow's kidney tastes quite amazing when you cook it properly. If you leave it in liquid or mushy, it will not taste good. On the other hand, when you fry it, it becomes delicious.

Serving Size: 2

Serving Size: 30 Minutes

Ingredients:

- 1 lb. cow kidney
- 1 tsp red chili powder
- 1 tsp cumin
- 1 tbsp oil
- 1 inch ginger root, minced
- 4 garlic cloves, minced
- 1 cup red onion, chopped
- 1 ½ tsp coriander powder
- 1 pinch of cinnamon powder
- 1 pinch of cardamom powder

- Salt to taste

- 1 tbsp soy sauce

- 1 tbsp BBQ sauce

- Fresh coriander, chopped, to serve

Instruction:

Clean the cow kidney. Cut it into small cubes.

In a pot add the cubed kidney. Pour 2 cup of water. Bring it to boil.

Drain and rinse off the kidney. Set aside.

In a large wok, heat the oil. Add the ginger, garlic and onion.

Cook for 5 minutes. Add the turmeric, cumin, salt, red chili powder, cardamom, cinnamon and coriander.

Stir for 2 minutes. Add the soy sauce, BBQ sauce and finally add the kidney.

Cook for 10 minutes. Serve hot with coriander on top.

Spicy Chorizo Shrimp Paella

Paella is one such dish that cannot go wrong. Men love it because it is super tasty and you do not need too much prep to make this wonderful dish.

Serving Size: 2

Serving Size: 30 Minutes

Ingredients:

- 1 cup rice
- ½ cup shrimp, cleaned, skin removed
- ½ cup sliced chorizo
- 2 cup fish stock
- Salt and pepper to taste
- 1 tsp mixed herbs
- ½ cup chopped scallion
- 1 tbsp soy sauce
- 2 tbsp warm milk
- ¼ tsp saffron

- Fresh parsley, chopped

- 2 tbsp oil

Instruction:

Soak the saffron in warm water for 10 minutes. Set aside.

In a large pot, add the oil. Add the chorizo and cook for 2 minutes.

Add the scallion, soy sauce, rice, and shrimp.

Toss for 2 minutes. Add the saffron mix, mixed herbs, salt,pepper, and fish stock.

Mix well and cover. Cook for 20 minutes. Add the parsly on top and serve hot.

Minced Chicken and Bean Chili

Have you ever tried making chili with two types of beans and minced chicken? It is quite a good combination.

Serving Size: 2

Serving Size: 30 Minutes

Ingredients:

- 1 can soybean, drained
- ½ cup minced chicken
- 1 onion, diced
- 1 can black bean, drained
- 1 tbsp lemon juice
- ½ cup tomato puree
- 1 tsp salt
- ½ tsp oregano
- 1 tsp paprika
- ¼ tsp turmeric

- 1 garlic clove, minced

- 2 tbsp oil

- 2 cup mushroom stock

- Fresh coriander to serve

- Lemon wedges to serve

Instruction:

In a large pot, heat the oil. Fry the garlic and onion.

Add the minced chicken and stir for 5 minutes.

Add the beans and toss for 5 minutes.

Add the paprika, turmeric, salt, pepper, mushroom stock, lemon juice and tomato puree.

Mix well and cook for 15 minutes. Serve hot with lemon wedges and coriander.

Pan fried Pineapple lemon Fish

If you like fish, you will love this recipe. It is simple but tastes quite interesting.

Serving Size: 2

Serving Size: 10 Minutes

Ingredients:

- 1 lb. whole fish
- 2 tbsp lemon juice
- 1 tsp chopped parsley
- 1 tsp paprika
- ¼ tsp turmeric
- ¼ tsp cumin
- Salt and pepper to taste
- 2 tbsp oil
- 1 tbsp pineapple juice
- 1 tsp sugar

Instruction:

Combine the pineapple juice, lemon juice, sugar, salt, pepper, paprika and turmeric.

Marinate the fish in the mixture.

In a pan heat the oil. Pan fry the fish for 5 minutes on each side.

Serve hot.

Beef Skewers

Skewers in any form tastes irresistible. But when you make it with beef and yogurt and BBQ sauce, it elevates the taste.

Serving Size: 2

Serving Size: 20 Minutes

Ingredients:

- 1lb boneless fat less beef
- 1 cup yogurt
- 1 tsp ginger powder
- 1 tsp garlic powder
- 1 tsp cumin
- 1 tsp pepper
- Salt to taste
- 1 tbsp BBQ sauce
- 2 tbsp oil

Instruction:

Cut the beef into small cubes.

Combine all the Ingredients in a bowl. Marinate the beef for 4 hours or longer.

Thread the marinated beef in the skewers.

Heat the grill and add oil to it.

Grill each side for 5 minutes. Serve hot.

Smoking Hot chicken Drumsticks

Men love chicken and they love spice. They love BBQ even more. This is a full proof recipe for men that cannot go wrong.

Serving Size: 2

Serving Size: 20 Minutes

Ingredients:

- 6 chicken drumsticks
- 1 tbsp soy sauce
- 1 tsp pepper
- 1 tsp red chili powder
- 1 tsp oil
- 1 tbsp BBQ sauce
- 1 tsp brown sugar

Instruction:

Combine the brown sugar, soy sauce, BBQ sauce, red chili powder, and pepper in a bowl.

Marinate the drumsticks in the mixture for 2 hours.

In the grill, add the oil. Grill the drumsticks until they are blackish in color.

Deep Fried Fish with Potato Fries

Deep fried potatoes with deep fried fish, life cannot be more delicious than this?

Serving Size: 2

Serving Size: 20 Minutes

Ingredients:

- 1 cup potatoes cut into sticks

- 1 whole fish

- 1 tsp red chili powder

- 1 tsp cumin

- Pepper to taste

- 1 tbsp fish sauce

- 1 pinch of turmeric

- Salt to taste

- Oil for deep frying

Instruction:

Deep fry the potatoes. Sprinkle some salt and pepper on top. Arrange on a serving plate.

Prepare the fish by discarding the intestines. Clean it properly.

Marinate the fish with salt, fish sauce, pepper, turmeric, cumin and red chili powder.

Deep fry the fish. Add to the serving plate. Serve hot.

Lemon Herby Grilled Salmon

Salmon is very good for our health. You can enjoy it in many ways. Grilling is one of the quickest ways to enjoy a delicious salmon fillet.

Serving Size: 2

Serving Size: 10 Minutes

Ingredients:

- 2 salmon fillets

- 1 tbsp lemon juice

- 1 tsp chopped parsley

- 1 tsp chopped chives

- Salt to taste

- Pepper to taste

- 1 tbsp butter

- Lemon slices to serve

- Fresh herbs, chopped, to serve

Instruction:

Debone the fish fillets. Marinate the fish using lemon juice, salt, pepper, chives and parsley.

In the grill add the butter. Add the fish and grill for 3 minutes per side.

Serve hot with herbs and lemon slices on top.

Beef Burger

Who does not love burger? Men love it with guilt-free feelings. This is a very basic beef burger but tastes very good.

Serving Size: 1

Serving Size: 10 Minutes

Ingredients:

- 1 beef patty
- 1 red chili, chopped
- 2 lettuce leaves
- ½ cup onion
- 1 tbsp BBQ sauce
- 1 tbsp tomato ketchup
- 1 cheese slice
- Oil for frying

Instruction:

Fry the patty brown for 3 minutes on each side.

Fry the onion golden brown.

Spread the BBQ sauce and tomato sauce onto the buns.

Assemble the burger with lettuce, red chili, fried onion, cheese and patty. Serve hot.

Beef Potato Broccoli Casserole

A casserole is a comfort food not only men but women also love. This particular casserole combined the goodness of minced beef with super-food broccoli and potatoes.

Serving Size: 2

Serving Size: 40 Minutes

Ingredients:

- 1 cup sliced potatoes

- 1 cup diced broccoli

- Fresh basil leaves

- 1 cup grated cheese

- 1 cup milk

- 1 tbsp flour

- Salt and pepper to taste

- 1 cup minced beef

- 1 tbsp oil

Instruction:

In a pan heat the oil. Fry the beef for 5 minutes.

Transfer to the casserole dish.

Preheat the oven to 400 degrees F.

Add the vegetables. Combine the milk, flour, salt, pepper and cheese. Mix well.

Add on top of the vegetables. Top with basil.

Bake for 40 minutes. Serve.

Beef Pepperoni Mushroom Pizza

Who doesn't love pizza? You can make your own special pizza at home if you invest a little time in the kitchen.

Serving Size: 2

Serving Size: 15 Minutes

Ingredients:

- 1 cup flour
- 1 tsp active dry yeast
- 1 tsp sugar
- ½ cup milk
- 2 tbsp oil
- 1 cup grated cheese
- 1/2cup sliced mushroom
- ½ cup beef pepperoni
- 2 tbsp pizza sauce
- 1 tbsp chopped black olives

- 2 tbsp chopped tomatoes

Instruction:

Combine the flour, yeast, salt, sugar and milk.

Add oil and knead for 5 minutes. Cover with a wet towel. Let it sit for 30 minutes.

Knead again and roll it out flat.

Spread the pizza sauce. Add the pepperoni, mushroom, cheese, tomato and black olives.

Bake for 15 minutes with 350 degrees F. Serve hot.

Spaghetti and Meatballs

Spaghetti and meatball has so many variations to it. You can choose any meat of your choice. You can make as spicy a sauce as you like. You can use different combination of cheese. Try this recipe and see how easy it is to make.

Serving Size: 2

Serving Size: 30 Minutes

Ingredients:

- 1 lb. spaghetti

- 1 cup minced beef

- 1 cup red onion, chopped

- Salt and pepper to taste

- 1 egg

- 1 tbsp corn flour

- 1 tbsp oil

- ½ cup tomato puree

- Fresh herbs, chopped

- 1 tbsp soy sauce

- 1 tbsp apple cider vinegar

- ½ cup grated cheese

Instruction:

Combine the minced beef, half the onion, chili, egg and corn flour.

Mix well and create meatballs. Fry the golden brown.

Boil the spaghetti for 8-10 minutes in salted water. Drain well.

In a pan heat the oil. Fry the onion for 2 minutes.

Add the tomato puree, salt, pepper, vinegar, soy sauce and 2 tbsp water.

Cook for 4 minutes. Add the fried meatballs. Toss for a minute.

Add the spaghetti. Cook for 2 minutes. Serve hot.

Conclusion

Let's end the fallacy that men rely on women to cook! If men want, they can cook equally good food as women. The choice of food may vary from women as men are drawn to meat slightly more than their opposite gender. Another difference is men usually opt for simple cooking, and this is what this book promises. Every single recipe here is easy to make and anyone can do this.

Author's Afterthoughts

THANK YOU

Thanks ever so much to each of my cherished readers for investing the time to read this book!

I know you could have picked from many other books, but you chose this one. So, a big thanks for downloading this book and reading all the way to the end.

If you enjoyed this book or received value from it, I'd like to ask you for a favor. Please take a few minutes to post an honest and heartfelt review on Amazon.com. Your support does make a difference and helps to benefit other people.

Thanks for your Reviews!

Rachael Rayner

About the Author

Rachael Rayner

Are you tired of cooking the same types of dishes over and over again? As a mother of not one, but two sets of twins, preparing meals became very challenging, very early on. Not only was it difficult to get enough time in the kitchen to prepare anything other than fried eggs, but I was constantly trying to please 4 little hungry mouths under 5 years old. Of course I would not trade my angels for anything in the world, but I had just about given up on cooking, when I had a genius idea one afternoon while I was napping beside one of my sons. I am so happy and proud to tell you that since then, my kitchen has become my sanctuary and my children have become my helpers. I have transformed my meal preparation, my grocery shopping habits, and my cooking style. I am Racheal Rayner, and I am proud to tell you that I am no longer the boring mom sous-chef people avoid. I am the house in our neighborhood where every kid (and parent) wants to come for dinner.

I was raised Jewish in a very traditional household, and I was not allowed in the kitchen that much. My mother cooked the same recipes day in day out, and salt and pepper were probably the extent of the seasonings we were able to detect in the dishes she made. We did not even know any better until we moved out of the house. My husband, Frank is a foodie. I thought I was too, until I met him. I mean I love food, but who doesn't right? He revolutionized my knowledge about cooking. He used to take over in the kitchen, because after all, we were a modern couple and both of us worked full time jobs. He prepared chilies, soups, chicken casseroles—one more delicious than the last. When I got pregnant with my first set of twins and had to stay home on bed rest, I took over the kitchen and it was a disaster. I tried so hard to find the right ingredients and recipes to make the dishes taste something close to my husband's. However, I hated follow recipes. You don't tell a pregnant woman that her food tastes bad, so Frank and I reluctantly ate the dishes I prepared on week days. Fortunately, he was the weekend chef.

After the birth of my first set of twins, I was too busy to even attempt to cook. Sure, I prepared thousands of bottles of milk and purees, but Frank and I ended up eating take out 4 days out of 5. Then, no break for this mom, I gave birth to my second set of twins only 19 months later! I knew that now it was not just about Frank and I anymore, but it was about these little ones for whom I wanted to cook healthy meals, and I had to learn how to cook.

One afternoon in March, when I got up from that power nap with my boys, I had figured out what I needed to do to improve my cooking skills and stop torturing my family with my bland dishes. I had to let go of everything I had learned, tasted, or seen from my childhood and start over. I spent a week organizing my kitchen, and I equipped myself a new blender. I also got some fun shaped cookie cutters, a rolling pin, wooden spatulas, mixing bowls, fruit cutters, and plenty of plastic storage containers. I was ready.

My oldest twins, Isabella and Sophia are now teenagers, and love to cook with their Mom when they are not too busy talking on the phone. My youngest twins Erick and John, are now 10 years old and so helpful in the kitchen, especially when it's time to make cookies.

Let me start sharing my tips, recipes, and shopping suggestions with you ladies and gentlemen. I did not reinvent the wheel here but I did make my kitchen my own, started storing my favorite baking ingredients, and visiting the fresh produce market more often. I have mastered the principles of slow cooking and chopping veggies ahead of time. I have even embraced the involvement of my little ones in the kitchen with me.

I never want to hear you say that you are too busy to cook some delicious and healthy dishes, because BUSY, is my middle name.

Printed in Great Britain
by Amazon